THE
JESUS
I NEVER KNEW

PARTICIPANT'S GUIDE

By Philip Yancey

The Jesus I Never Knew

What's So Amazing About Grace?

The Bible Jesus Read

Reaching for the Invisible God

Where Is God When It Hurts?

Disappointment with God

The Student Bible, General Edition (with Tim Stafford)

Meet the Bible (with Brenda Quinn)

Church: Why Bother?

Finding God in Unexpected Places

I Was Just Wondering

Soul Survivor

Rumors of Another World

Prayer: Does It Make Any Difference?

Keeping Company with God: A Prayer Journal

By Philip Yancey and Dr. Paul Brand

Fearfully and Wonderfully Made

In His Image

The Gift of Pain

In the Likeness of God

PHILIP YANCEY

THE JESUS I NEVER KNEW

PARTICIPANT'S GUIDE

WRITTEN BY GREG CLOUSE AND SHERYL MOON

SIX SESSIONS ON THE LIFE OF CHRIST

ZONDERVAN®

ZONDERVAN.com/
AUTHORTRACKER
follow your favorite authors

We want to hear from you. Please send your comments about this book to us in care of zreview@zondervan.com. Thank you.

ZONDERVAN®

The Jesus I Never Knew Participant's Guide
Copyright © 1998, 2008 by Philip D. Yancey

Requests for information should be addressed to:
Zondervan, *Grand Rapids, Michigan* 49530

ISBN 978-0-310-27530-5

Interior design by Beth Shagene

Printed in the United States of America

08 09 10 11 12 13 • 25 24 23 22 21 20 19 18 17 16 15 14 13 12 11 10 9 8 7 6 5 4 3 2 1

CONTENTS

INTRODUCTION

Philip Yancey's study of Jesus began with a class he taught at LaSalle Street Church in Chicago. The use of movies about the life of Jesus, the discussion from class members, and his personal study all combined to give him a new view of Jesus—hence the title of his bestselling book *The Jesus I Never Knew*.

Yet all along he had another goal in mind: He wanted his quest for Jesus to serve as a guide for other people. As Yancey himself wrote, "In the end, what does it matter if a reader learns about 'The Jesus Philip Yancey Never Knew'? What matters infinitely more is for *you* to get to know Jesus."

You are about to engage in a six-session study that is bound to change your perceptions of who Jesus is. (NOTE: The first edition of this curriculum, published ten years ago, featured fourteen sessions, but this new, streamlined version covers the same general ground and is more user-friendly, especially for small groups.) Each week you will see several film depictions of Jesus, his life and his ministry. Some will be funny, some will be profound, and some will even be disturbing. After reacting to the film clips you will turn to the Gospel accounts of these same scenes and discuss what you believe really happened. Obviously the filmmakers used their own interpretations of what happened. The film clips are there to help us think about Jesus in a new way—to examine our own preconceived ideas in comparison with what the Bible teaches.

For those who have been raised in the church and have known Jesus all of their lives, *and* for those who are meeting Jesus for the first time, Philip Yancey challenges us to think about this man as the Bible presents him—brilliant, creative, challenging, fearless, compassionate, unpredictable, and ultimately satisfying. We hope you will find that the DVD clips combined with the Bible study and your own discussion will help you to discover the Jesus *you* never knew!

THE JESUS
I THOUGHT I KNEW

*The more I studied Jesus,
the more difficult it became to pigeonhole him. . . .
As [theologian] Walter Wink has said, if Jesus had never lived,
we would not have been able to invent him.*
THE JESUS I NEVER KNEW, P. 23

INTRODUCTION (8 MINUTES)

DVD Introduction by Philip Yancey

Questions to Think About

- In your mind's eye, what did Jesus look like? Where did you get this picture of him (films, paintings, books, Sunday school)? Can you describe specific images from the past?

- If you met someone from another religion or culture, how would you answer their question: Who is this man, Jesus?

GROUP DISCOVERY (44 MINUTES)

DVD Teaching Notes

As you listen to Philip Yancey and watch the scenes from these four films, use the space provided to note anything that stands out to you.

King of Kings

The Gospel According to St. Matthew

Son of Man

Jesus of Nazareth

DVD Discussion

1. Compare the Jesuses of the first three movie clips. Which one most appeals to you? Which one least appeals to you? Which one seems most biblically accurate?

2. Why do we, like these movie producers, often "make" Jesus into what we want him to be?

3. What types of things muddy our perceptions of the real Jesus?

4. Reread the following quote by Philip Yancey from the DVD:

> Jesus was born not in Rome, the seat of power, but in tiny
> Bethlehem. He grew up not in Jerusalem, the center of religion, but
> in Galilee, the butt of country-bumpkin jokes.... Jesus was born
> in Asia, like half of all babies born today. He spent several years
> as a refugee in Africa, where many refugees have lived. Poverty, a
> refugee, a minority race, living in occupied territories ... those were
> the choices God made and the kinds of people Jesus would love so
> much.

What does this tell us about God? How should these facts
encourage us? How might they alter our perspective?

Bible Exploration

Could it be true, this Bethlehem story of a Creator descending to be born on one small planet? If so, it is a story like no other. Never again need we wonder whether what happens on this dirty little tennis ball of a planet matters to the rest of the universe. Little wonder a choir of angels broke out in spontaneous song, disturbing not only a few shepherds but the entire universe.

The Jesus I Never Knew, p. 45

---

1. We often forget that people in Jesus' day had no clearer picture of him than we do today. Read Mark 6:1–6 and John 7:40–43. What do these passages tell us?

2. Read the following passages and note what each says about who Jesus is and what he's really like:

   • Matthew 11:28–30

- Luke 19:10

- John 2:13–16

- Philippians 2:6–8

- Colossians 1:15–20

3. Read Luke 2:1–20, probably the most well-known Gospel account of Jesus' birth. How does this rendering compare with what gets emphasized about Christmas today? Which aspect of the story seems most surprising to you? Why?

WRAP-UP (5 MINUTES)

DVD Wrap-up by Philip Yancey

Closing Group Question

If time permits, take a minute or two to respond to this question: What one new thing did you discover in this session about the "unexpected Messiah"?

No one who meets Jesus ever stays the same. I have found that the doubts that afflict me from many sources — from science, from comparative religion, from an innate defect of skepticism, from aversion to the church — take on a new light when I bring them to the man named Jesus.

The Jesus I Never Knew, p. 25

KNOWING JESUS:
A PERSONAL JOURNEY TO DO ON YOUR OWN

Between sessions, consider any or all of the following questions. Also, if possible, read chapters 1–5 of the book *The Jesus I Never Knew*, which covers the content from session one as well as additional material about Jesus' early life and the start of his ministry.

1. Read Matthew 1:18–25 and Luke 1:26–38, in which angels foretell Jesus' birth to Joseph and Mary, respectively. Put yourself in the place of Joseph or Mary. How would you have responded to the angels' announcements? How do you think you would have responded to Joseph and Mary's situation if you were a member of their extended family?

2. Read Luke 2:41–52. In what ways do you think Jesus was a typical child? In what ways was he different?

3. Read about Satan's tempting of Jesus in Luke 4:1 – 13. What do you learn about the nature of temptation in this passage? What do you learn from Jesus about how to respond to temptation?

4. What scares you most about getting to know the real Jesus? What excites you most? Have you put Jesus in a box? How?

THE BEATITUDES AND SERMON ON THE MOUNT

To put the issue bluntly, are the Beatitudes true?
If so, why doesn't the church encourage poverty and mourning
and meekness and persecution instead of striving against them?
What is the real meaning of the Beatitudes,
this cryptic ethical core of Jesus' teaching?
THE JESUS I NEVER KNEW, P. 109

INTRODUCTION (5 MINUTES)

DVD Introduction by Philip Yancey

Questions to Think About

- How do you deal with Jesus' baffling teachings, like the Beatitudes, his words that began the Sermon on the Mount?

- Why might people consider such messages hard to accept, even offensive?

GROUP DISCOVERY (49 MINUTES)

DVD Teaching Notes

As you listen to Philip Yancey and watch the scenes from these four films, use the space provided to note anything that stands out to you.

Gospel Road

The *Jesus* film

Son of Man

The Gospel According to St. Matthew

DVD Discussion

If the Sermon on the Mount sets forth God's standard of holiness ... I may as well resign from the start. The Sermon on the Mount did not help me improve; it simply revealed all the ways I had not.

The Jesus I Never Knew, p. 136

1. In what way(s) did the movie clips help you better envision how revolutionary and controversial Jesus' words would have sounded to his original hearers? Would you consider yourself "lucky" to be included among those he calls blessed? Why or why not?

2. Can people who hold the Gospels in high esteem justify *not* taking the Beatitudes literally or with full seriousness? What does it mean for readers, bottom line, to take these sayings of Jesus at face value?

3. Discuss Philip Yancey's comment from the DVD presentation: "God's ideal is so high that you'll never be able to reach it, no matter how strict your legalism ... but God's grace is so amazing that you don't have to."

4. We often criticize the legalism of the first-century Pharisees. Name a few forms of legalism of which some twenty-first-century Christians might be guilty. Why do you think such people are blind to these actions/attitudes?

Bible Exploration

Human beings do not readily admit desperation. When they do, the kingdom of heaven draws near.

The Jesus I Never Knew, p. 117

1. Reread the Beatitudes in Matthew 5:3–12. What hope would Jesus' audience, living under Roman oppression, have found in these words? Do you think western Christians today would find more rebuke than hope in them? Why or why not?

2. What do the Beatitudes teach us about God's sense of justice? of God's idea of success? of God's desired pattern for living?

3. Jesus' Sermon on the Mount takes up three chapters in Matthew's gospel and covers a spectrum of practical, everyday topics. From the following list, collectively choose up to four topics; read the related verses; then answer the subsequent questions for each on pages 28–31.

Matthew 5:13–16	Salt and Light
Matthew 5:17–20	The Law
Matthew 5:21–26	Anger
Matthew 5:27–30	Lust
Matthew 5:31–32	Divorce
Matthew 5:33–37	Vows
Matthew 5:38–42	Retaliation
Matthew 5:43–48	Loving Enemies
Matthew 6:1–4	Giving to the Needy
Matthew 6:5–15	Prayer
Matthew 6:16–18	Fasting
Matthew 6:19–24	Money
Matthew 6:25–34	Worry
Matthew 7:1–6	Criticizing Others
Matthew 7:7–12	Asking, Seeking, Knocking
Matthew 7:13–14	Way to Heaven
Matthew 7:15–23	Fruit in People's Lives
Matthew 7:24–28	People Who Build Houses on Rock and Sand

Selected Topic #1 _____

How do you think this passage sounded to those who first heard it? Why might it be startling or even offensive to those who read it today?

What does this passage teach us about God and eternal values?

How does this passage apply in today's settings?

Selected Topic #2

How do you think this passage sounded to those who first heard it? Why might it be startling or even offensive to those who read it today?

What does this passage teach us about God and eternal values?

How does this passage apply in today's settings?

Selected Topic #3 _____

How do you think this passage sounded to those who first heard it? Why might it be startling or even offensive to those who read it today?

What does this passage teach us about God and eternal values?

How does this passage apply in today's settings?

Selected Topic #4 _____

How do you think this passage sounded to those who first heard it? Why might it be startling or even offensive to those who read it today?

What does this passage teach us about God and eternal values?

How does this passage apply in today's settings?

WRAP-UP (5 MINUTES)

DVD Wrap-up by Philip Yancey

Closing Group Question

If time permits, take a minute or two to respond to this question: What one new thing did you discover in this session about Jesus' teachings?

The worst tragedy would be to turn the Sermon on the Mount into another form of legalism; it should rather put an end to all legalism.

The Jesus I Never Knew, p. 144

KNOWING JESUS:
A PERSONAL JOURNEY TO DO ON YOUR OWN

Between sessions, consider any or all of the following questions. Also, if possible, read chapters 6 – 7 of the book *The Jesus I Never Knew*, which covers the content from session two.

1. Study as many other topics/passages from "Bible Exploration" question 3 as you would like. (You may need some extra notebook paper!)

2. The Lord's Prayer (Matthew 6:9–13; see also Luke 11:1–4) is considered by many a "model" prayer. Review it phrase by phrase and note what you discover about God, his values, and our priorities.

Praying the Lord's Prayer, Phrase by Phrase

Like most churchgoers I have prayed the Lord's Prayer hundreds of times, so that I say it without even thinking. It helps me to slow down, reflect on each phrase, and even add my own personal application.

Our Father, who art in heaven

I begin with an endearing term of relationship, "Father." Remind me today that you live and reign, not in heaven only but all around me and in my life. Make me aware of your active presence all day, in all my undertakings and in the people I meet.

Hallowed be your name

How can I recognize you—in the splendor of nature, in the odd mix of people I meet, in the still voice that calls me to be more like you? May I "hallow" what lies before me, by consciously referring it to you, and also honor your perfection, your holiness, by seeking to become more like you.

Your kingdom come

Yes, and allow me to be an agent of that kingdom by bringing peace to the anxious, grace to the needy, and your love to all whom I touch. May people believe in your reign of goodness because of how I live today.

Your will be done on earth as it is in heaven

I see that will most clearly in Jesus, who healed the sick and comforted the grieving, who lifted up the downtrodden, who stood always for life and not death, for hope and not despair, for freedom and not bondage. He lived out heaven's will on earth. Help me be like Jesus.

Give us today our daily bread

We have no guarantee of a day beyond this one. May I trust you for what I need today, nourishment for both body and soul, and not worry about future needs and wants. May I also be ever responsive to those who lack bread today.

Forgive us our debts, as we also have forgiven our debtors

Remind me of my true state, as a debtor who can never buy my way into your favor. Thank God, I do not have to. Grant me the same attitude of forgiving grace toward those who owe me, and who have wronged me, that you show toward me.

And lead us not into temptation,
but deliver us from the evil one

Let me not slide mindlessly toward evil today. Make me alert to its temptations and strong to resist it, with neither fear nor regret.

Philip Yancey, *Prayer: Does It Make Any Difference?*
(Zondervan, 2006), pp. 171–172

3. Read the "Personalized Beatitudes" below. How do these statements reflect your values and behaviors? Choose one or two that you especially need to think and pray about.

- I am blessed because in my loneliness, my fears, and my inner struggles, God has promised me a beautiful future. That promise helps me see my struggles with new eyes.

- I am blessed as I grieve. In the depths of my sorrow Jesus meets me and mourns with me, bringing comfort in unexpected ways.

- I am blessed choosing not to exalt myself. This means I get overlooked at times, but I'm living for God, not for the acclaim of men and women. Someday I'll be glad I chose the way of humility.

- I am blessed in my yearning to live as Jesus did. God is faithful to me as I ponder Jesus' righteous ways and pray for the Spirit to guide how I live and who I am.

- I am blessed because I choose to show mercy, even when others don't really deserve it. I see much in me that is undeserving, yet Jesus has been merciful again and again.

- I am blessed because I'm careful about what I do, see, read, and think about. I want to be pure because this is when I can see God most clearly. This is when I am closest to God.

- I am blessed because I long for peace among those around me. I desire to enter into the world of others to better understand and come alongside them. I'm willing to do what is uncomfortable for the sake of peace, following in the footsteps of Jesus.

- I am blessed when because of my loyalty to Jesus, others look down on me, violate my God-given rights, lie about me with evil intent, or hurt me. This world is not my home, and persecution blesses me because it is a reminder of the kingdom of heaven that awaits me not so far away. For "no eye has seen, no ear has heard, no mind has conceived what God has prepared for those who love him" (1 Corinthians 2:9).

4. It's much easier to study God's laws and tell others to obey them than to put them into practice. How are *you* doing at obeying God? When do you keep God's *rules* but close your eyes to God's *intent*?

A REVOLUTION OF GRACE

How did Jesus, the only perfect person in history,
manage to attract the notoriously imperfect?
And what keeps us from following in his steps today?
THE JESUS I NEVER KNEW, P. 148

INTRODUCTION (5 MINUTES)

DVD Introduction by Philip Yancey

Questions to Think About

- Can you think of individuals or groups who are considered "outcasts" in the Bible?

- Which individuals or groups are sometimes considered "outcasts" in our world today?

GROUP DISCOVERY (46 MINUTES)

DVD Teaching Notes

As you listen to Philip Yancey and watch the scenes from these two films, use the space provided to note anything that stands out to you.

Jesus of Nazareth

Gospel Road

DVD Discussion

> Jesus moved the emphasis from God's holiness (exclusive) to God's mercy (inclusive). Instead of the message "No undesirables allowed," he proclaimed, "In God's kingdom there are no undesirables."
>
> *The Jesus I Never Knew*, p. 155

1. What character qualities of Jesus seem evident to you in the two movie clips? How would you characterize his hearers in the clips (the Pharisee's guests in the *Jesus of Nazareth* clip; the woman caught in adultery as well as her accusers in the *Gospel Road* clip)?

2. Philip Yancey noted in the DVD presentation that, for the most part, Jesus attracted not the good, upstanding, righteous people of his day (the Pharisees), but the ungodly, unrighteous, undesirable people (prostitutes, tax collectors, Roman centurions, those with leprosy). How does that compare to the

types of people the church generally attracts today? Why do you think that is so?

What would it take to change this situation? And would you meet resistance if you tried? (If a real-life scenario will help generate discussion, imagine inviting a notorious sinner or social outcast to worship at your church. How would he or she be received? How would you be received?)

Why don't sinners like being around Christians and the church today?

3. In the DVD presentation, Yancey quoted a former prostitute who said, "When you're at the bottom and have no one to look down on, you may just look up and hold out your hands for help." What is it about being needy—physically, emotionally, financially, spiritually—that makes a person more open to receiving assistance? Do you think it's easy for Christians to admit they still have needs? Why or why not?

4. What makes it so difficult to be a grace-receiver?

Bible Exploration

1. Read Matthew 9:9–13, the Gospel account of Jesus eating at the home of Matthew, shortly after this hated tax collector had decided to follow Jesus. What do you think it was about Jesus that convinced Matthew to "change professions," as it were, as well as to invite many of his tax collector friends to meet this Galilean rabbi?

What do you suppose Jesus was driving at when he told the contemptuous Pharisees, "I desire mercy, not sacrifice"?

2. Jesus' parable of the prodigal son (recounted in the DVD) is a popular depiction of God's grace to the undeserving. Read the last portion of the story—the homecoming scene (Luke 15:18–32)—and concentrate on the words and actions of the three main characters: the father (as grace-giver), the younger son (as grace-receiver), and the older son (as grace-denier).

With which character do you most identify? Why?

Why is pride an enemy of grace? Who chose to swallow their pride in this story? Who didn't?

How do you think the Pharisees hearing Jesus' story would have understood it? How would the tax collectors and "sinners" have understood it?

3. Interestingly, the Gospels never record Jesus using the word "grace," though he certainly both embodied and demonstrated it. Read John 1:17, and then briefly compare and contrast law and grace, especially as they relate to what's been discussed thus far.

What, in your own words, is the grace of Jesus Christ and how can we receive it?

WRAP-UP (5 MINUTES)

DVD Wrap-up by Philip Yancey

Closing Group Question

If time permits, take a minute or two to repond to this question: What one new thing did you discover in this session about the grace of Jesus?

Grace introduces a new world of logic. Because God loves the poor, the suffering, the persecuted, so should we. Because God sees no undesirables, neither should we. By his own example, Jesus challenged us to look at the world through ... "grace-healed eyes."

The Jesus I Never Knew, p. 155

KNOWING JESUS:
A PERSONAL JOURNEY TO DO ON YOUR OWN

Between sessions, consider any or all of the following questions. Also, if possible, read chapter 8 of the book *The Jesus I Never Knew*, which covers the content from session three.

1. Read John 8:1–11, the gospel account re-created in Johnny Cash's film *Gospel Road*, shown during the session. Note both Jesus' verbal and nonverbal communication in this incident—to the woman *and* to the teachers of the law and the Pharisees. Do you think the woman felt forgiven even though Jesus did not say so with words? With what did Jesus balance his lack of condemnation?

Do you agree with the current saying, "Condemn the sin, not the sinner"? Is that really possible? Why or why not?

2. Read Hebrews 4:14–16. Note what this encouraging passage says about Jesus, about his approachability, about grace. (These would be excellent verses to memorize.)

3. Think about your own ability to give grace. Are there particular individuals or groups of individuals with whom you struggle in this area? Now think about your ability to receive God's grace. Are there areas of your life in which you cling to your own reputation and good works? Are there any areas in which you will not or are not able to accept God's forgiveness? Be receptive to whatever God is telling you.

JESUS' MIRACLES

Jesus never met a disease he could not cure,
a birth defect he could not reverse,
a demon he could not exorcise.
But he did meet skeptics he could not convince
and sinners he could not convert.
Forgiveness of sins requires an act of will on the receiver's part,
and some who heard Jesus' strongest words about grace
and forgiveness turned away unrepentant.

THE JESUS I NEVER KNEW, PP. 174–175

INTRODUCTION (6 MINUTES)

DVD Introduction by Philip Yancey

Questions to Think About

• Why do you think Jesus performed miracles?

• Has your adult view of miracles changed from your childhood view? In what way, if any?

GROUP DISCOVERY (45 MINUTES)

DVD Teaching Notes

As you listen to Philip Yancey and watch the scenes from these three films, use the space provided to note anything that stands out to you.

Heaven

The *Jesus* film

Gospel Road

DVD Discussion

1. Philip Yancey uses the first movie clip to contrast Jesus' ministry style with that considered typical, by skeptics at least, of many Christians today. Imagine if Jesus had used miracles simply to show off his power and force God on people. Wouldn't a few more public, large-scale miracles have gotten greater attention from the Jewish and Roman leaders and better established Jesus' credibility? What does it say about God that Jesus did not act in that manner?

2. Put yourself in the sandals of the man Jesus healed of blindness, as depicted in the final two movie clips. What would it have been like to see for the first time ever? How would you explain it to friends and family? How would it change the rest of your life? Could you have obeyed Jesus' command not to tell anyone about the healing, as he regularly instructed?

3. In the DVD presentation, Philip Yancey says that we know how God feels about our pain because we know how Jesus responded to people he encountered who were in pain. How does this biblical reality help you cope with your own hurts and minister to the hurts of others? Discuss briefly Yancey's statement: "Jesus' miracles were a sign of how the world should be and one day will be."

4. Why do you think we don't see more miracles today?

I have spent much of my adult life coming to terms with questions first stirred up during my youth. Prayer, I have found, does not work like a vending machine: insert request, receive answer. Miracles are just that, *miracles*, not "ordinaries" common to daily experience. My view of Jesus has changed too. As I now reflect on his life, miracles play a less prominent role than what I had imagined as a child. Superman, he was not.

The Jesus I Never Knew, p. 166

Bible Exploration

1. The Gospels record Jesus performing about three dozen
   miracles, depending on how you count them. As a group,
   select two miracles from the following list; read the Scripture
   passage; then answer the subsequent questions.

Matthew 14:15–21	Feeding of the 5,000
Matthew 9:20–22	Healing of the bleeding woman
Matthew 8:28–34	Demons sent into the pigs
Mark 9:14–29	Healing of the boy with an evil spirit
Luke 17:11–19	Healing of the ten with leprosy
John 2:1–11	Wine at the wedding of Cana

Selected Miracle #1 _____

What does this passage tell you about Jesus?

What kind of impact did this miracle have on those
around the situation at the time: family, friends, the crowd,
the religious leaders? Is there any indication that people

acknowledged Jesus as the Messiah because of this miracle?
Or is there any indication that people's faith was increased?

Why do you think Jesus chose to do this particular miracle?

Does Jesus still work miracles of this sort in similar situations?
What is usually the outcome if this type of miracle does
occur? What *might* be the outcome if it did?

Selected Miracle #2 _____

What does this passage tell you about Jesus?

What kind of impact did this miracle have on those around the situation at the time: family, friends, the crowd, the religious leaders? Is there any indication that people acknowledged Jesus as the Messiah because of this miracle? Or is there any indication that people's faith was increased?

Why do you think Jesus chose to do this particular miracle?

Does Jesus still work miracles of this sort in similar situations? What is usually the outcome if this type of miracle does occur? What *might* be the outcome if it did?

2. Though the Gospels record two other incidents of Jesus raising the dead (the widow of Nain's son, Luke 7:11–15; Jairus's daughter, Luke 8:40–56), the raising of Lazarus seems pivotal, because it was after this resurrection in Bethany that the Jewish leaders began in earnest their plot to kill Jesus. Read John 11:1–48, the account of the miracle and its aftermath, then discuss the next questions:

Jesus performed this miracle for reasons other than to bring back to life a dear friend. Look at verses 4, 14–15, and 40–42. What do you learn about his purpose?

The concept of belief in Jesus comes up again and again in this passage. Observe the various responses:

• Jesus' disciples

• Mary and Martha

• The other people at Lazarus's tomb

• The chief priest and Pharisees

Note evidences of Jesus' compassion in this passage. How would you respond to those who argue that Jesus could have saved this family their suffering by coming more swiftly to Lazarus's aid?

What does it say about the nature of miracles and the nature of earthly existence to realize that Lazarus would ultimately die again? (See also John 12:10.) On the other hand, what do miracles tell us about God's ultimate plan?

How interesting that the Jewish religious leaders acknowledged Jesus was performing miraculous signs, yet refused to accept his authenticity (see verses 46–48). Philip Yancey says, "A sign is not the same thing as proof; a sign is merely a marker for someone who is looking in the right direction." Why did the religious leaders choose not to believe? Why do you think some people today make that same decision against Jesus, while others see the same "signs" and believe?

WRAP-UP (6 MINUTES)

DVD Wrap-up by Philip Yancey

Closing Group Question

If time permits, take a minute or two to respond to this question: What one new thing did you discover in this session about Jesus' miracles and/or why he performed them?

Every physical healing [Jesus did] pointed back to a time in Eden when physical bodies did not go blind, get crippled, or bleed nonstop for twelve years—and also pointed forward to a time of re-creation to come. The miracles he did perform, breaking as they did the chains of sickness and death, give me a glimpse of what the world was meant to be and instill hope that one day God will right its wrongs. To put it mildly, God is no more satisfied with this earth than we are; Jesus' miracles offer a hint at what God intends to do about it.

The Jesus I Never Knew, p. 182

KNOWING JESUS:
A PERSONAL JOURNEY TO DO ON YOUR OWN

Between sessions, consider any or all of the following questions. Also, if possible, read chapter 9 of the book *The Jesus I Never Knew*, which covers the content of session four.

1. Study as many other miracles/passages from "Bible Exploration" question 1 as you would like. (You'll likely need more notebook paper for your observations.)

2. A survey of the book of Acts reveals that miracles, like the ones Jesus performed, were regular occurrences in the early church. Read Acts 3, the account of Peter healing the crippled beggar, and answer the following questions:

By whose power did Peter heal?

What opportunity did the miracle give Peter?

Scan Acts 4 and list the repercussions of the miracle, both negative and positive.

Why do you think miracles continued so regularly during this period following Jesus' departure to heaven?

3. As you read the rest of Acts, you discover other occasions when the disciples performed miracles, occasions when God directly performed the miraculous on the disciples' behalf, and occasions when there was apparently no intervention at all. Complete the following chart for a sampling of incidents. Then spend some time evaluating your findings, especially what you conclude about God's methods.

Bible Passage	What Happened?	Who Intervened?
Acts 6:8–14; 7:54–60		
Acts 9:32–41		
Acts 12:1–11		
Acts 13:50; 14:19		

Bible Passage	What Happened?	Who Intervened?
Acts 16:16–18		
Acts 16:22–28		
Acts 20:7–12		
Acts 28:1–6		

4. Consider the following possible explanations for both biblical miracles and those that have occurred since:

- Magic
- God's answer to human prayer
- Proof that Jesus was God
- The Devil's power
- A sign of how the world was meant to be
- Exaggerated stories
- The antidote to human pain
- Jesus' opportunity to show he cared

Which of these explanations hold credence for you and why? How important are Jesus' miracles to your personal faith?

JESUS' DEATH AND RESURRECTION

Despite the shame and sadness of it all,
somehow what took place on a hill called Calvary
became arguably the most important fact of Jesus' life —
for the writers of the Gospels and Epistles, for the church,
and, as far as we can speculate, for God as well.

THE JESUS I NEVER KNEW, P. 202

INTRODUCTION (5 MINUTES)

DVD Introduction by Philip Yancey

Questions to Think About

- Which of the events leading up to Good Friday hold most significance for you?

- Why do you think the Gospel writers devoted a relatively small percentage of space to Jesus' history-changing Easter resurrection?

GROUP DISCOVERY (45 MINUTES)

DVD Teaching Notes

As you listen to Philip Yancey and watch the scenes from these three films, use the space provided to note anything that stands out to you.

From the Manger to the Cross

Gospel Road

King of Kings

DVD Discussion

1. Imagine yourself as one of Jesus' disciples who witnessed the scenes depicted in this session's movie clips. What would you have felt watching the torture and death of the one whom you had followed and on whom you had pinned your hopes? What would you have done in the aftermath of the crucifixion?

2. Now imagine yourself as one of the Jewish religious leaders who had plotted Jesus' death, once rumors of his resurrection spread. How would you have felt? What would you have done?

3. In the DVD presentation, Philip Yancey notes that almost a third of the content of the Gospels centers on the tragedy of Jesus' last week on earth. What do these accounts of Jesus'

pain and heartache tell us about God? Why would Jesus endure such abuse and suffering?

4. Have you ever felt like one of Jesus' disciples, stuck in the bewildering Saturday between Good Friday and Easter Sunday? Explain the situation and how God may have made his presence known to you in that in-between time.

Here at the cross is the man who loves his enemies, the man whose righteousness is greater than that of the Pharisees, who being rich became poor, who gives his robe to those who took his cloak, who prays for those who despitefully use him. The cross is not a detour or hurdle on the way to the kingdom, nor is it even the way to the kingdom; it is the kingdom come.

John Howard Yoder, quoted in *The Jesus I Never Knew*, p. 196

Bible Exploration

1. The following chart traces primary events of Holy Week. Read the Bible passage for each event, then briefly describe the scene, its significance, and Jesus' demeanor in the midst of it.

Event/Passage	Scene
Triumphal Entry (Luke 19:28–44)	
Jesus in the Temple (Luke 19:45–47)	
The Last Supper (Matthew 26:26–29)	
Jesus in Gethsemane (Matthew 26:36–46)	
Jesus on Trial (Matthew 26:57–27:2, 11–13)	
The Crucifixion (Matthew 27:31–56)	

Significance	Jesus' Demeanor

Considering as a whole Jesus' attitudes, actions, and reactions throughout the whirlwind of Holy Week events, what stands out to you?

2. Read Luke 18:31–34. What do verses 31–33 say about Jesus' identity? What do they say about his determination to do the Father's will?

How did the disciples respond to Jesus' words (v. 34)? How would you explain their lack of understanding? God's mercy? Ignorance or unwillingness on their part? A misinterpretation of Jesus' mission?

3. Read Mark 16:1–8. What images of this account of the resurrection impact you? Does the matter-of-factness of Mark's description surprise you at all? Why or why not?

If time allows, compare Mark's rendering with the account in John 20:1–18.

No theologian can adequately explain the nature of what took place within the Trinity on that day at Calvary. All we have is a cry of pain from a child who felt forsaken.... We are not told what God the Father cried out at that moment. We can only imagine.

The Jesus I Never Knew, pp. 201–202

WRAP-UP (5 MINUTES)

DVD Wrap-up by Philip Yancey

Closing Group Question

If time permits, take a minute or two to respond to this question: What one new thing did you discover about Jesus in this session?

We who read the Gospels from the other side of Easter, who have the day printed on our calendars, forget how *hard* it was for the disciples to believe.

The Jesus I Never Knew, p. 214

KNOWING JESUS:
A PERSONAL JOURNEY TO DO
ON YOUR OWN

Between sessions, consider any or all of the following questions. Also, if possible, read chapters 10–11 of the book *The Jesus I Never Knew*, which covers the content from session five.

1. Another memorable scene from Holy Week was Jesus washing the disciples' feet. Read the account in John 13:1–17 (John is the only Gospel writer to record it), then answer the following questions:

   What is the context of this event? (Compare John 13:21–27 with Matthew 26:20–29 if you need help chronologically placing it.)

   What similarities do you find in these two upper room events?

What lessons do you find in Jesus' act of footwashing? in Peter's response? in your own willingness or lack thereof to behave as Jesus did?

2. It is amazing to consider Jesus' thorough concentration on ministry at the beginning of Holy Week, given that he knew what lay ahead. He taught often, both publicly (in the temple) and privately (to his disciples in what has come to be known as the Upper Room Discourse). Read the Upper Room Discourse (John 14–17) and note the words of Jesus that encourage you specifically today.

3. During this session's "Bible Exploration," you read about Jesus' resurrection appearance to the women outside the empty tomb. Now read about three other post-resurrection appearances: to two unnamed disciples on the road to Emmaus (Luke 24:13–35), to the disciples in the upper room (Luke 24:36–49), and to Thomas (John 20:24–29). What differences do you see between Jesus' pre- and post-resurrection body? What about him is unchanged?

With which person/people group from among these followers (including the women) do you most identify? Why?

4. In your own words, write what Jesus' death and resurrection mean to you. How is this belief reflected in your everyday life?

THE DIFFERENCE
JESUS MAKES

—⟨⟨⟨⟨⟩⟩⟩⟩—

How can an unholy assortment of men
and women be the body of Christ?
I answer with a different question:
How can one sinful man, myself,
be accepted as a child of God?
One miracle makes possible the other.
THE JESUS I NEVER KNEW, PP. 235–236

INTRODUCTION (5 MINUTES)

DVD Introduction by Philip Yancey

Questions to Think About

- Have you ever wondered why God's plan didn't include Jesus staying on earth instead of ascending to heaven?

- What sounds more appealing—Jesus *beside* you or the Holy Spirit *in* you? Why?

GROUP DISCOVERY (46 MINUTES)

DVD Teaching Notes

As you listen to Philip Yancey and watch the scenes from these three films, use the space provided to note anything that stands out to you.

The Gospel According to St. Matthew

Son of Man

The *Jesus* film

DVD Discussion

1. Think back to the movie clips you just viewed and put
   yourself in the place of a first-century follower of Jesus left
   behind following his ascension. How would you have felt?
   What would have kept you going? For comparison sake, think
   of a time you had to say good-bye to someone you really cared
   about.

2. If Jesus could foresee such disasters as the Crusades, the
   Inquisition, the Christian slave trade, and apartheid, why did
   he ascend in the first place? Why does the church, the body of
   Christ, so faintly resemble him?

3. In the DVD presentation, Philip Yancey called Jesus' plan for spreading his message the "dandelion method." What could this multiplication strategy achieve that Jesus could not accomplish on his own? How do you fit into this divine plan? your church? your small group?

Jesus left few traces of himself on earth. He wrote no books or even pamphlets. A wanderer, he left no home or even belongings that could be enshrined in a museum. He did not marry, settle down, and begin a dynasty. We would, in fact, know nothing about him except for the traces he left in human beings. That was his design.

The Jesus I Never Knew, p. 228

Bible Exploration

1. Read Luke's two accounts of Jesus' ascension and the days preceding it in Luke 24:50–53 and Acts 1:1–11. Also briefly skim John 21. Then answer the following questions:

   What kinds of things did Jesus do in the forty days between his resurrection and ascension?

   What was Jesus' primary instruction to his disciples at this time? (See Acts 1:4–5, 7–8.)

How did the disciples respond to Jesus' post-resurrection appearances? How would they have been encouraged by Jesus' parting words? How would they have been encouraged by the angels' words (Acts 1:11)?

2. Jesus consistently taught about his kingdom, sometimes directly and sometimes in parables. Read the following passages, complete the chart, then answer the subsequent questions.

Bible Passage	Jesus' Teaching about the Kingdom
Matthew 13:24–30, 36–43	
Matthew 24:4–14	
John 18:36–37	

Why are Jesus' teachings so hard to grasp?

How do his teachings go against what we often *hear* about the kingdom of God? What distortions of the kingdom, if any, have you heard?

3. Read 1 Corinthians 12:12–26 and discuss what it means to be the body of Christ. What are the privileges and responsibilities of this God-given assignment?

Sheep among wolves, a tiny seed in the garden, yeast in bread dough, salt in meat: Jesus' own metaphors of the kingdom describe a kind of "secret force" that works from within. He said nothing of a triumphant church sharing power with authorities. The kingdom of God appears to work best as a minority movement, in opposition to the kingdom of the world. When it grows beyond that, the kingdom subtly changes in nature.

The Jesus I Never Knew, p. 246

WRAP-UP (4 MINUTES)

DVD Wrap-up by Philip Yancey

Closing Group Question

If time permits, take a minute or two to discuss this question:
What one new thing did you learn about Jesus in this session?

Jesus is radically unlike anyone else who has ever lived. The difference, in [English novelist and theologian] Charles Williams' phrase, is the difference between "one who is an example of living and one who is the life itself."

The Jesus I Never Knew, p. 258

KNOWING JESUS:
A PERSONAL JOURNEY TO DO ON YOUR OWN

In the coming days, consider any or all of the following questions. Also, if possible, read chapters 12–14 of the book *The Jesus I Never Knew*, which covers the content of session six.

1. Choosing how to respond to the resurrected Jesus is always a personal decision—both now and in the first century. Read Matthew 28, which describes the events of Easter morning and beyond from various perspectives. How did the women and other disciples respond? How did the Jewish religious leaders and Roman soldiers respond? How did Jesus respond to people's belief or lack thereof?

2. Another parable of the kingdom is found in Matthew 21:28–32 (read verses 23–27 for the context). What do you learn about the kingdom from this story? What do you learn about Jesus' expectation for those who desire to follow him? What can the contemporary church learn from this parable?

3. Use Galatians 2:20 to describe what it means to live as a representative of Jesus in the world today. What do we give up? What do we gain?

4. Though Jesus bodily left the earth at his ascension, he did not leave us to fend for ourselves. Read the following passages about the Holy Spirit's role in the life of a Christian and note anything that stands out to you.

- John 14:25–26

- John 16:7–15

- Romans 8:1–27

- 1 Corinthians 2:6–13

- Galatians 5:16–25

5. Did your perceptions of Jesus change at all over the course of this six-session study? If so, how? And how will your life be different because of your discoveries?

3 More DVD Curriculums from Philip Yancey

What's So Amazing About Grace?

(10 sessions)

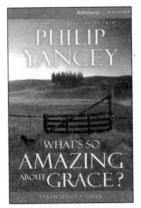

If grace is God's love for the undeserving, what does it look like in action? And if Christians are its sole dispensers, then how are we doing at lavishing grace on a world that knows far more of cruelty and unforgiveness than it does of mercy?

Small Group Edition DVD with Leader's Guide 0-310-26179-1
Participant's Guide 0-310-23325-9

The Bible Jesus Read

(8 sessions)

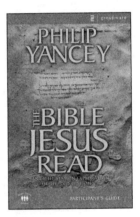

Philip Yancey serves as guide and interpreter of five sometimes shocking and cryptic writings of the Old Testament—Job, Deuteronomy, Psalms, Ecclesiastes, and the Prophets—to help small groups members get to know God better.

Small Group Edition DVD with Leader's Guide 0-310-27521-0
Participant's Guide 0-310-24185-5

Prayer: Does It Make Any Difference?

(6 sessions)

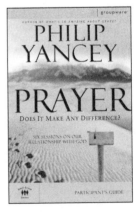

Philip Yancey helps you and your small group explore and experience the very heartbeat of our relationship with God: prayer. What is prayer? How does it work? And more importantly, does it work?

Small Group Edition DVD with Leader's Guide 0-310-27525-3
Participant's Guide 0-310-27527-X